RIANS

by Louise Armstrong
Consultant: Alison Howard

How to use this book

Each topic in this book is clearly labelled and contains all these components:

Topic heading

Introduction to the topic

Sub-topic 1 offers complete information about one aspect of the topic

Words in capitals are explained in the Glossary

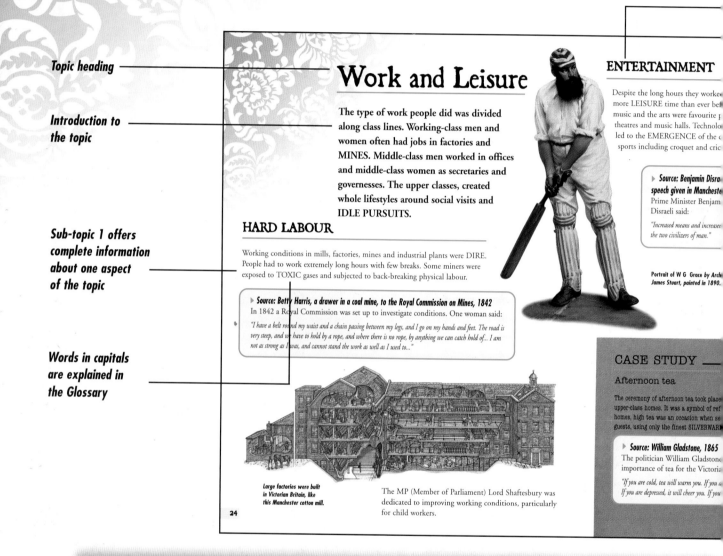

Work and Leisure

The type of work people did was divided along class lines. Working-class men and women often had jobs in factories and MINES. Middle-class men worked in offices and middle-class women as secretaries and governesses. The upper classes, created whole lifestyles around social visits and IDLE PURSUITS.

HARD LABOUR

Working conditions in mills, factories, mines and industrial plants were DIRE. People had to work extremely long hours with few breaks. Some miners were exposed to TOXIC gases and subjected to back-breaking physical labour.

▶ **Source: Betty Harris, a drawer in a coal mine, to the Royal Commission on Mines, 1842**
In 1842 a Royal Commission was set up to investigate conditions. One woman said:

"I have a belt round my waist and a chain passing between my legs, and I go on my hands and feet. The road is very steep, and we have to hold by a rope, and where there is no rope, by anything we can catch hold of... I am not as strong as I was, and cannot stand the work as well as I used to..."

Large factories were built in Victorian Britain, like this Manchester cotton mill.

24

The MP (Member of Parliament) Lord Shaftesbury was dedicated to improving working conditions, particularly for child workers.

ENTERTAINMENT

Despite the long hours they worked more LEISURE time than ever bef music and the arts were favourite p theatres and music halls. Technolo led to the EMERGENCE of the c sports including croquet and cric

▶ **Source: Benjamin Disra speech given in Manchester**
Prime Minister Benjam Disraeli said:

"Increased means and increased the two civilizers of man."

Portrait of W G Grace by Arch James Stuart, painted in 1890.

CASE STUDY

Afternoon tea

The ceremony of afternoon tea took place upper-class homes. It was a symbol of ref homes, high tea was an occasion when se guests, using only the finest SILVERWAR

▶ **Source: William Gladstone, 1865**
The politician William Gladstone importance of tea for the Victoria

"If you are cold, tea will warm you. If you a If you are depressed, it will cheer you. If you

ISBN 978 1 84898 074 7
This edition published in 2009 by *ticktock* Media Ltd
Printed in China
9 8 7 6 5 4 3 2 1
A CIP catalogue record for this book is available from the British Library.

Copyright © *ticktock* Entertainment Ltd 2005. First published in Great Britain in 2005 by *ticktock* Media Ltd, The Old Sawmill, 103 Goods Station Road, Tunbridge Wells, Kent, TN1 2DP.

Sub-topic 2 offers complete information about one aspect of the topic

Some suggested words to use in your project

The Glossary explains the meaning of any unusual or difficult words appearing on these two pages

Words to use in your project

excursion – a pleasure trip
exploitation – taking advantage of someone or something
industrious – hard-working
legislation – a law
recreation – fun
refreshments – food and drink

Glossary

dire – very bad
emergence – the beginning
idle – avoiding work; lazy
leisure – free time
mine – an underground works where coal and precious metals are gathered
pursuits – hobbies
silverware – tableware made of silver
toxic – poisonous

See also: The Empire 6–7; Society 10–11; Literature 14–15; Art and Crafts 20–21

Other pages in the book that relate to what you have read here are listed in this bar

The Case Study is a closer look at a famous person, artefact or building that relates to the topic

Afternoon tea for a middle-class Victorian family.

25

Captions clearly explain what is in the picture

Each photo or illustration is described and discussed in its accompanying text

CONTENTS

The Victorians

Queen Victoria reigned in Britain from 1837 to 1901. The Victorian era was a time of rapid changes and developments in the arts and sciences. Literature, medicine, education, architecture, transportation, technology and industry also progressed dramatically. There was an economic boom, making England a world leader.

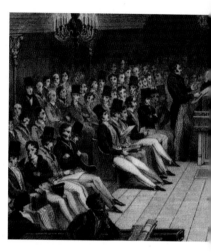

A print of the House of Commons.

QUEEN VICTORIA

Alexandrina Victoria was the only child of Edward, Duke of Kent, fourth son of King George III. She became queen at 18, when her uncle George IV died. In 1840, she married her German cousin, Prince Albert. Their 20-year marriage produced nine children. In 1861, Albert died of TYPHOID. Victoria was devastated, and for ten years, she withdrew from public life.

Victoria's Golden Jubilee in 1887 brought the RECLUSIVE queen out of isolation, and she once again embraced public life. Victoria died on 22 January 1901.

A portrait of Victoria by Heinrich von Angeli.

> ▶ **Source: The letters of Queen Victoria, 20 December 1861**
> After Albert's death, Victoria wrote to her uncle King Leopold of Belgium:
>
> *"… to be cut off in the prime of life … cut off at forty-two – when I had hoped with such INSTINCTIVE certainty that God never would part us, and would let us grow old together … it is too awful, too cruel!"*

4

PARLIAMENT

The Reform Act of 1832 gave the power of making laws to the House of Lords, and EXECUTIVE AUTHORITY to the House of Commons. The queen had no direct input in policy decisions. When Victoria became queen, Lord Melbourne was prime minister. While Melbourne was liked and trusted by the queen, Victoria did not like his successor Lord Palmerston, who was elected prime minister in 1855.

▶ **Source: The diary of Queen Victoria**
When Lord Palmerston died, Victoria wrote:

"We had, God knows! terrible trouble with him about Foreign Affairs. Still, as Prime Minister he managed affairs at home well, and behaved to me well. But I never liked him."

Words to use in your project

acrimonious – *unfriendly*
approval – *consent*
confinement – *being locked away indoors*
decorum – *good behaviour*
diarist – *one who keeps a diary*
enamoured – *fond of*
peerage – *the rank of nobility*
reconciliation – *a restoration to friendship*
secret ballot – *a vote cast secretly*

Glossary

authority – *having the right to command*
executive – *empowered and required to administer*
instinctive – *spontaneous or natural*
mentor – *a teacher or coach*
reclusive – *preferring to live alone*
stroke – *a sudden attack caused by lack of blood flow to the brain*
typhoid – *an infectious fever*

See also: The Empire 6–7; Society 10–11; Significant People 18–19; Work and Leisure 24–25

CASE STUDY

Lord Melbourne

Lord Melbourne (William Lamb) was born on 15 March 1779. Melbourne was prime minister briefly in 1834, and again from 1835 to 1841. When Victoria came to the throne, he became a MENTOR to the young queen. Melbourne died of a STROKE on 24 November 1848.

▶ **Source: The diary of Queen Victoria**
Victoria's feelings for Melbourne were expressed in her journal:

"He is such an honest, good kind-hearted man and is my friend, I know it."

Lord Melbourne was prime minister when Victoria became queen in 1837.

The Empire

Under Queen Victoria the British Empire reached its ZENITH and many people believe that England was at its best during Victorian times. British technology, commerce, language and government spread throughout the empire, which covered roughly a quarter of the world.

EXPANSION

During the Victorian period Britain conquered many countries, including Egypt in 1881, Canada in 1867 and India in 1876. Many Victorians opposed IMPERIALISM because they saw it as oppressive to the cultures of acquired countries, but statesman Earl Grey believed the British Empire was the best hope for the civilization of the world.

▶ **Source: Earl Grey, The Colonial Policy of Lord John Russell's Administration, *1853***
In 1853, Earl Grey wrote:

"The authority of the British crown is at this moment the most powerful instrument, under Providence, of maintaining peace and order in many extensive regions of the earth, and thereby assists in diffusing amongst millions of the human race, the blessing of Christianity and civilization."

This map shows the extent of the British Empire (coloured orange) in 1886.

INDUSTRIALIZATION

Britain's Industrial REVOLUTION reached its height during the Victorian era. It quickly became a country of industrialized towns, factories, mines and workshops. By 1900, 80 per cent of the population lived in cities. The massive migration to cities and towns caused the rise of SLUMS and cramped housing.

> ▶ **Source: Arnold Toynbee, The Industrial Revolution in England, 1884**
> Historian and social reformer Arnold Toynbee said:
>
> "... the industrial England of today is not only one of external conditions. Side by side with the revolution ... there has taken place a change no less radical in men's ECONOMIC principles, and in the attitude of the State to individual enterprise..."

Rail travel increased dramatically in the Victorian era.

Words to use in your project

conservatism – *the traditional nature of something*
constitutional – *a way of ruling a state by a set of principles*
evolve – *to change naturally*
indomitable – *impossible to subdue or defeat*
legislation – *a law*
liberalism – *open-mindedness*
seclusion – *being away from other people*

Glossary

economic – *relating to financial matters*
imperialism – *a policy of extending a country's power*
industries – *businesses that produce things*
metropolis – *a large, busy city*
revolution – *a complete change*
slums – *unpleasant, overcrowded areas, inhabited by the poor*
zenith – *the highest point*

See also: The Victorians 4–5; Work and Leisure 24–25; At Home 28–29

CASE STUDY

Victorian London

London was a city of startling contrasts. The population grew rapidly in the 19th century to more than six million. New building developments and INDUSTRIES were set against overcrowded slums.

> ▶ **Source: The Morning Chronicle, 19 October 1849**
> Henry Mayhew described London:
>
> "... the METROPOLIS covered an extent of nearly 45,000 acres, and contained upwards of two hundred and sixty thousand houses, occupied by one million eight hundred and twenty thousand souls..."

The River Thames was clogged with ships and London had more shipyards than anywhere on the globe.

View over the Houses of Parliament and the River Thames in Victorian times.

Religion

The Victorian era brought numerous challenges to Christianity. Supporters of evolutionary theories, including Charles Darwin, criticized the Bible, and new sects of Christianity developed. New churches were built to cope with the expanding population and missionaries were sent to the British colonies to CONVERT local people to Christianity.

CHRISTIAN VALUES

For rich and poor alike, the church was the centre of English life, but the dominance of the Church of England led to DISSENTING groups. The principal religious groups of 19th-century England were Methodist, Baptist, Congregationalist, Unitarian and Quaker. While all these sects shared the Christian DOCTRINE, each had its own interpretation of the Bible. Many religious sects felt that the only way to improve society was to convert everybody to their beliefs. Some people saw this as hypocritical. The Church of England and other groups were PROFESSING to help the poor, while simply exploiting desperate people, imposing judgements and a sense of guilt that made their lives even more miserable. Charles Darwin wrote:

"If the misery of our poor be caused not by the laws of nature, but by our institutions, great is our sin."

Victorians were appalled by Darwin's theory that man descended from apes.

CHRISTIANITY

In Victorian England, religion was thought to be a remedy for all that was wrong with the world.

The Oxford Movement led the HIGH CHURCH campaign.

▶ **Source: John Henry Newman, in a speech upon becoming a cardinal, 1879**

John Henry Newman, founder of the pro-Catholic Oxford Movement, said:

"For thirty, forty, fifty years I have resisted to the best of my powers the spirit of liberalism in religion. Never did Holy Church need champions against it more sorely than now."

Many new churches were built in urban areas, but church attendance was highest in RURAL villages.

Words to use in your project

disillusioned – *left feeling disappointed or dissatisfied*
evangelist – *one who tries to convert others to Christianity*
puritan – *a person committed to morals and religion*
theologians – *people who study religion*

Glossary

convert – *to change religions*
dissenting – *holding a different opinion to the majority*
doctrine – *a belief or principle*
High Church – *the belief that the rituals of the Anglican Church should be similar to those of the Roman Catholic Church*
professing – *claiming*
rural – *relating to the countryside*

See also: The Empire 6–7; Education 12–13; Architecture 16–17; Art and Crafts 20–21

CASE STUDY

Westminster Abbey

The Collegiate Church of St Peter in London is also known as Westminster Abbey. Many royal marriages and funerals have taken place there, and it has been used as a coronation church since William the Conqueror was crowned there in 1066. Victoria was crowned at Westminster Abbey on 28 June 1838.

▶ **Source: The diary of Queen Victoria**

In her diary, Victoria wrote:

"I reached the Abbey amid deafening cheers ... I was then seated upon St Edward's chair ... the Crown being placed on my head; which was, I must own, a beautiful, impressive moment."

Westminster Abbey was extensively restored in the Victorian era.

Society

Victorian society was structured according to classes: upper class, upper middle class, lower middle class and working class. Very poor people were the underclass. The upper class included the ARISTOCRACY. The middle classes protested against a society that rewarded INHERITED privilege, and strove to create a position for themselves.

UPPER AND MIDDLE CLASS

The 19th century was a time of great social change. Class divisions were marked by distinctions in dress, speech, social behaviour and ETIQUETTE. The upper classes were the main employers and had the greatest wealth. The middle classes had great social and economic influence. They ranged from lawyers, doctors, factory owners and bankers to shopkeepers and clerks. The working classes had a wide range of manual and service occupations.

William Makepeace Thackeray's novel *Vanity Fair* was about the moral decay and selfishness of Victorian society.

> ▶ **Source: William Makepeace Thackeray, Vanity Fair, 1847**
> This is how Thackeray described one of his characters:
>
> *"Whenever he met a great man he GROVELLED before him as only a free-born Briton can do."*

Wealth, possessions and a GENTEEL lifestyle were important to the Victorians.

POOR AND WORKING CLASS

The increased acceptance of the working classes led to the 1867 Reform Act, which extended the vote to more than 60 per cent of men. Despite the economic expansion of the Industrial Revolution, living conditions for the poor were APPALLING.

> ▶ **Source: Thomas Carlyle, Past and Present – 'Midas' [The Condition of England], 1843**
>
> Thomas Carlyle, a social observer, noted:
>
> *"It is not to die, or even to die of hunger, that makes a man WRETCHED; many men have died; all men must die, … it is to die slowly all our life long, imprisoned in a deaf, dead, Infinite Injustice …"*

Poor working-class parents often forced children as young as four years old to work.

Children were often put to work at a very young age.

CASE STUDY

Lord Shaftesbury

Anthony Ashley Cooper was a Member of Parliament who developed an interest in social issues. He became the leader of the factory reform movement, and the 1833 Factory Act was passed by Parliament on Cooper's proposals. In 1840, he pushed through an act that prevented small boys being used as chimney sweeps.

> ▶ **Source: Lord Shaftesbury's speech to the House of Commons, 4 August 1840**
>
> *"The future hopes of a country must, under God, be laid in the character and condition of its children …"*

Anthony Ashley Cooper, 7th Earl of Shaftesbury.

Education

Upper-class children were often educated at home with a view to preparing them for university. Middle-class children who were not taught at home usually went to private schools. Working-class children attended schools, which usually had just one large classroom.

EDUCATION AT HOME

GOVERNESSES were women who taught upper- and middle-class children in their homes. Many governesses were quite well educated and the job was one of few considered suitable for middle-class women. Many young upper-class children were taught by their mothers.

Children could be beaten if they did not learn their lessons.

> ▶ **Source: Josephine Butler, An Autobiographical Memoir, 1913**
> Josephine Butler, who was born in 1828, tells of the experience in her AUTOBIOGRAPHY:
>
> *"In the pre-educational era (for women at least), we had none of the advantages which girls of the present day have. We owed much to our dear mother, who was very firm in requiring from us that whatever we did should be thoroughly done ..."*

SCHOOLS

A Victorian 'ragged school' from the 1840s.

Parents who had a little money to spare sent their children to school. Young children were often sent to DAME schools, usually run by untrained women, while older children went to day schools. Other schools, called 'RAGGED' schools, were organized by churches and CHARITIES. The school day typically lasted from 9am to 12.30pm and then from 2pm to 4.30pm. Schooling had to be paid for throughout most of the 19th century, though more relaxed laws were later introduced.

▶ Source: 1870 Education Act

The 1870 Education Act stated:

"The country would be divided into about 2500 school districts; ...own by-laws which would allow them to charge fees or, if they wanted, to let children in free."

CASE STUDY

Public school logs

Most schools kept a LOGBOOK to record punishments given to children and the teachers' comments.

▶ Source: Milton House Public School log, 1881

April 8th - One death during week from Fever. Every member of Craig family ill with Fever and removed to hospital.
May 13th - Universally large number of TRUANTS. Parents of found summoned before the School Board tomorrow.
November 25th - Sent for Mrs Ferguson, New Street. Ordered her to take home her daughter and clean her head, which is overrun with VERMIN. This has escaped notice till now as the girl had a bandage over her head.

An entry from a Victorian school logbook (1882).

Literature

British writers produced some of their greatest literature during the 19th century. It was also a time when women came to be more accepted as novelists and poets. Most highly regarded authors had received an upper-middle-class education.

POETRY

Many poets of the Victorian age were concerned with exploring social, political and religious issues of the time. The poetry of Robert Browning and his wife, Elizabeth Barrett Browning, was immensely popular, while Rudyard Kipling's work captured the spirit of the lives of British soldiers during the expansion of the empire.

William Blake, Samuel Taylor Coleridge, William Wordsworth, Lord Byron and John Keats were among many poets who wrote in the Romantic style. Romanticism was a movement that flourished during the 19th century, and was embraced by poets, philosophers and artists.

> ▶ **Source: William Wordsworth, 'Written in Early Spring', in Palgrave's Golden Treasury, 1875**
> Wordsworth explored many Romantic themes and ideas, as in the following poem:
>
> *"The birds around me hopp'd and play'd, Their thought I cannot measure, But the least MOTION which they made It seemed a thrill of pleasure."*

Alfred, Lord Tennyson, was one of the greatest poets of the Victorian era and a POET LAUREATE.

THE VICTORIAN NOVEL

The English novel became very popular in Victorian times. The novels of Charles Dickens were full of accurate PORTRAYALS of URBAN life. William Makepeace Thackeray was another novelist of the time.

> ### ▶ Source: Emily Brontë, Wuthering Heights, 1847
> Emily Brontë's *Wuthering Heights* told about people experiencing strong emotions:
>
> *"I've stayed here and been beaten like a dog, abused and cursed and driven mad, but I stayed just to be near you, even as a dog."*

Another important writer was Thomas Hardy, whose novels captured the spirit of times that were being lost to progress.

A scene from Mira Nair's 2004 film adaptation of Thackeray's novel Vanity Fair.

Words to use in your project

contemporary – *happening now or in the same time period*
epitomize – *to describe something perfectly*
interact – *to communicate*
introspective – *quiet and thoughtful*
monologue – *a long speech or piece of text by one person*
nonconformist – *a person who does not comply with rules or laws*
perpetual – *permanent*

Glossary

idealizing – *showing something in a perfect form*
motion – *movement*
Poet Laureate – *a country's official poet*
portrayals – *depictions in a work of art or literature*
urban – *relating to towns and cities*

See also: Society 10–11; Art and Crafts 20–21; Work and Leisure 24–25; At Home 28–29

CASE STUDY

Children's literature

The Romantic movement also influenced books written for children, IDEALIZING childhood and conjuring other worlds and strange creatures. Distinguished writers of children's fiction included Robert Louis Stevenson and Edward Lear.

> ### ▶ Source: Lewis Carroll, Alice Through the Looking Glass, 1871
> Lewis Carroll is best known for his classic *Alice in Wonderland*. This is an extract from the sequel:
>
> *"Who are you?" said the caterpillar. This was not an encouraging opening for a conversation. Alice replied rather shyly: "I ... hardly know sir, just at present ..."*

The writer Lewis Carroll.

Architecture

Victorian architecture is notable for its massive scale and elaborate designs. Styles of classical periods provided inspiration and mixed with the new technology of the Industrial Revolution. The people's new-found love of design led to more creative and ORNATE architecture.

The huge water lilies at Kew Gardens.

VICTORIAN BUILDINGS

During the Victorian period there was a REVIVAL of many classical architectural styles. The Greek Revival (1825–1850) inspired the inclusion of columns. The Gothic Revival (1840 onwards) reproduced the intricate detailing of Tudor buildings. Italianate and Queen Anne styles were also popular. Many existing buildings were reconstructed to incorporate this embellishment including the Houses of Parliament. The MASS construction of buildings and mass production of furniture were made possible by industrialization. However, many people complained that these new methods created results that were too perfect and cut out individual craftsmen.

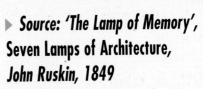

The Houses of Parliament were RECONSTRUCTED during the Victorian era.

> ▶ **Source: 'The Lamp of Memory', Seven Lamps of Architecture, John Ruskin, 1849**
> Victorian art and social critic John Ruskin wrote:
>
> *"Better the rudest work that tells a story or records a fact, than the richest without meaning."* (section 7)
> *"When we build, let us think that we build forever."* (section 10)

GARDENS

During the 19th century, neatly tended and ABUNDANT flower gardens and parks were fashionable. An impressive garden was a reflection of REFINEMENT and status, and it required taste and planning. For the first time, government funds were made available for the creation of public gardens across Britain. In 1841, the Royal Botanical Gardens at Kew, London opened to the public, with the striking Palm House created in 1848. For the Victorians, gardening was a way to create order and to connect with nature, but for others it was an art form.

▶ **Source: Sir Walter Scott, Essay on Landscape Gardening**
Sir Walter Scott wrote:

"Nothing is more completely the child of art than a garden."

Words to use in your project

artisan – *a skilled manual worker*
horticulture – *the art of gardening*
intricate – *elaborate*
modernism – *new ideas, methods and styles*
restoration – *the process of returning something to a former condition*

Glossary

abundant – *present in large quantities*
mass – *relating to large numbers*
ornate – *very decorative*
reconstructed – *rebuilt*
refinement – *elegance and sophistication*
revival – *something becoming popular again*

See also: The Empire 6–7; Society 10–11; Literature 14–15; Art and Crafts 20–21

CASE STUDY

Tower Bridge

For hundreds of years, London Bridge was the only crossing over the River Thames. By the 19th century, east London was so densely populated that people demanded a new crossing. The Special Bridge or Subway Committee was formed in 1876, and more than 50 designs were put forward for consideration. In 1884, a design by Horace Jones and John Wolfe-Barry was chosen. The construction of the bridge, which opens to allow tall vessels through, took eight years. It was given the name Tower Bridge because it is near the Tower of London.

A view of Tower Bridge, London.

Significant People

During the Victorian era some exceptional people made large contributions to literature, art, medicine, science, architecture, transportation and politics. For the first time, women began to be appreciated achievers in their own right, though it was not until the following century that they would be allowed to vote.

FAMOUS VICTORIANS

Famous Victorians came from all walks of life. The engineer Isambard Kingdom Brunel designed the Clifton Suspension Bridge, the Great Western Railway and the SS *Great Eastern*. Benjamin Disraeli was Britain's first Jewish prime minister. He brought India and the Suez Canal under control of the Crown.

> ▶ **Source: Benjamin Disraeli, speech**
> This quote sums up Disraeli's political style:
>
> *"Action may not always bring happiness; but there is no happiness without action."*

William Gladstone was prime minister four times. A religious man, he considered a career in the church before becoming a politician. David Livingstone was an explorer, CARTOGRAPHER and missionary who made three long EXPLORATIONS of East Africa.

This bronze statue of Isambard Kingdom Brunel overlooks the River Thames at Temple, London.

UNCONVENTIONAL WOMEN

For centuries, marriage and having children were considered the main purpose of women. During the Victorian era, many women began to fight for the same rights as men. Elizabeth Garrett Anderson was the first British female doctor. She founded a hospital for poor women and children in London. Anne Knight, who was a QUAKER, took an active role in the anti-slavery and TEMPERANCE campaigns.

Women suffragettes campaign for the right to vote.

> ▶ **Source: Anne Knight, leaflet that is believed to be the first call for women's SUFFRAGE, 1847**
>
> Knight fought for the women's suffrage movements, and in 1847 published a groundbreaking leaflet:
>
> *"Never will the nations of the earth be well governed until both sexes, as well as all parties, are fully represented … and a hand in the enactment and administration of the laws."*

Words to use in your project

aristocracy – *the privileged class of society*
domesticity – *the devotion to home and family life*
generation – *all the people born and living at the same time*
genteel – *courteous*
gentry – *high society*
unique – *the only one of its kind*

Glossary

cartographer – *a map maker*
enunciate – *to state a belief or theory clearly*
explorations – *distant journeys*
pioneer – *one of the first to do something*
Quaker – *a member of the Religious Society of Friends, devoted to peace*
suffrage – *the right to vote*
temperance – *anti-alcohol*

See also: The Victorians 4–5; Literature 14–15; Health and Medicine 26–27; Work and Leisure 24–25

CASE STUDY

Florence Nightingale

Florence Nightingale was a PIONEER of nursing. Nightingale and her team of 38 nurses volunteered to tend wounded soldiers in the Crimean War (1854–56) where the lamp she carried at night earned her the nickname 'The Lady with the Lamp'.

> ▶ **Source: Florence Nightingale, Notes on Hospitals, 1859**
>
> Nightingale's eagerness to improve conditions in hospitals fuelled a lifelong campaign. She wrote:
>
> *"It may seem a strange principle to ENUNCIATE as the very first requirements of a hospital: that it should do the sick no harm."*

Portrait of Florence Nightingale by an unknown artist.

Art and Crafts

During Victorian times, art became something that could be enjoyed by everyone, rather than just the privileged few. The many different styles of art and music that emerged catered for a wide variety of tastes and also tackled issues of concern at the time. Photography was also widely explored and practised.

ART AND CRAFTS

Various schools of art emerged, including Neoclassicism, Romanticism, Impressionism, post-Impressionism and the Pre-Raphaelite movement. Many artists painted IDYLLIC landscapes and country scenes. Classicism was influenced by ancient Greek and Roman architecture. Romanticism paid tribute to emotions, often using bold, bright colours. The Pre-Raphaelite movement was a style of art that PRECEDED the work of the RENAISSANCE painter Raphael. The Pre-Raphaelites painted people so true to life that they often looked like photographs. The Victorian era saw the founding of many public libraries, museums and art galleries that helped to make cultural pursuits available for everyone.

The Mirror of Venus, by Sir Edward Coley Burne-Jones, 1898.

MUSIC

Much of the music that the Victorians listened to, including old songs, hymns and concert music, was serious and conservative, offering views on politics and culture. OPERETTAS also became popular, due to the talents of Gilbert and Sullivan – particularly Gilbert's witty lyrics. Music halls involved lively singing and dancing and loud audience participation.

Marie Lloyd was a popular music-hall entertainer.

> ▶ **Source: G W Hunt, from 'Macdermott's War Song', 1878**
>
> The music halls provided opportunity for social comment, as in this song written during the 1878 Balkan crisis:
>
> *"We don't want to fight, but BY JINGO if we do … We've got the ships, we've got the men, and we've got the money too!"*

See also: Architecture 16–17; Clothes and Jewellery 22–23; Work and Leisure 24–25

Words to use in your project

aesthetic – *concerned with beauty*
graphic – *relating to visual art*
incorporate – *to include something as part or a whole*
masterpiece – *an outstanding work of art*
portray – *to show something visually in a work of art*
reminisce – *to remember past events with enjoyment*
rustic – *relating to the country*

Glossary

by jingo – *a mild swear word*
ennoble – *to give greater dignity*
idyllic – *perfect and unspoilt*
operettas – *short operas*
post-mortem – *after death*
preceded – *came before*
Renaissance – *an art movement of the 14th–16th centuries*

CASE STUDY

Photography

Initially, photography was regarded as a way of recording important events like birth, marriage and even death. Early cameras took a long time to capture an image, so people who posed had to stay still for several minutes. Victorian photographs, such as those of Julia Margaret Cameron, transformed photography into an art form.

> ▶ **Source: Julia Margaret Cameron, Annals of My Glass House, 1874**
>
> *"My aspirations are to ENNOBLE photography and to secure it for the character and uses of high art."*

POST-MORTEM photographs were also taken, intended to comfort bereaved relatives.

'The Mammalian Room' is by Frederick York, 1875.

Clothes and Jewellery

Fashion for women ranged from simple day dresses to elaborate evening gowns. Working-class people wore plain clothing, while upper-class women wore clothes made from delicate fabrics and expensive ribbon. Middle-class women copied upper-class dress.

FASHION AND COSTUME

Victorian women wore modest clothing that covered the entire body, with high lace-up boots and gloves and hats. Corsets were used to create a tiny waist. Men of all classes wore trousers, a shirt and a formal coat, often with a waistcoat. Hats varied according to class: working-class men wore caps, middle-class men wore derbys and the upper classes wore top hats. Children of both sexes wore dresses up to the age of six, when boys were put into BREECHES, shirts and jackets.

A lady's fan, made in about 1885.

> ▶ **Source: Thomas Carlyle, Sartor Resartus, 1834**
>
> Thomas Carlyle wrote a book about clothes:
>
> *"The first purpose of Clothes ... was not warmth or decency, but ornament ... Warmth he [the primitive human being] found in the toils of the chase; or amid dried leaves, in his hollow tree, in his bark shed, or natural grotto: but for Decoration he must have Clothes."*

JEWELLERY

Victorian jewellery included brooches, necklaces, rings, bracelets, lockets, CAMEOS, hair pins and combs. After Prince Albert's death, Queen Victoria abandoned precious jewels in favour of items made of black jet. This began a huge fashion for MOURNING jewellery, which was often set with a lock of a dead person's hair. Mass production of jewellery also began, though it was of a low quality.

A Victorian brooch, with a heart-shaped amethyst set in a cut diamond border.

See also: Art and Craft 20–21; At Home 28–29

CASE STUDY

Hairstyles

In early Victorian times, hair was usually worn parted in the middle and pulled smooth over the temples. In the 1850s, large coils of hair were held back with black or coloured silk nets. In the 1860s, the CHIGNON, or French twist, became popular, often accompanied by loops and BRAIDS of hair. From the 1870s, hair at the back of the head was sometimes worn loose. In the 1880s, a simpler style known as the Gibson Girl or Psyche knot became popular and hair was swept into a high knot on top of the head.

This photograph shows an elaborate Victorian hairstyle.

Work and Leisure

The type of work people did was divided along class lines. Working-class men and women often had jobs in factories and MINES. Middle-class men worked in offices and middle-class women as secretaries and governesses. The upper classes created whole lifestyles around social visits and IDLE PURSUITS.

HARD LABOUR

Working conditions in mills, factories, mines and industrial plants were DIRE. People had to work extremely long hours with few breaks. Some miners were exposed to TOXIC gases and subjected to back-breaking physical labour.

> ▶ **Source: Betty Harris, a drawer in a coal mine, to the Royal Commission on Mines, 1842**
> In 1842 a Royal Commission was set up to investigate conditions. One woman said:
>
> *"I have a belt round my waist and a chain passing between my legs, and I go on my hands and feet. The road is very steep, and we have to hold by a rope, and where there is no rope, by anything we can catch hold of … I am not as strong as I was, and cannot stand the work as well as I used to …"*

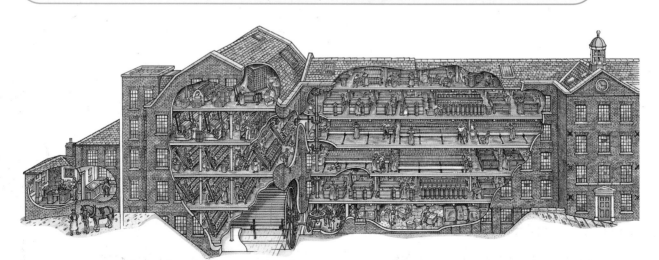

Large factories were built in Victorian Britain, like this Manchester cotton mill.

The MP (Member of Parliament) Lord Shaftesbury was dedicated to improving working conditions, particularly for child workers, who were often subjected to the same conditions as adult workers.

ENTERTAINMENT

Despite the long hours they worked, Victorians had more LEISURE time than ever before. Reading, music and the arts were favourite pastimes, as were theatres and music halls. Technological advances led to the EMERGENCE of the cinema and sports including croquet and cricket.

> ▶ **Source: Benjamin Disraeli, from a speech given in Manchester, 1872**
> Prime Minister Benjamin Disraeli said:
>
> *"Increased means and increased leisure are the two civilizers of man."*

Portrait of W G Grace *by Archibald James Stuart, painted in 1890.*

Words to use in your project

excursion – *a pleasure trip*
exploitation – *taking advantage of someone or something*
industrious – *hard-working*
legislation – *a law*
recreation – *an enjoyable activity*
refreshments – *food and drink*

Glossary

dire – *very bad*
emergence – *the beginning*
idle – *avoiding work; lazy*
leisure – *free time*
mine – *an underground works where coal and precious metals are gathered*
pursuits – *hobbies*
silverware – *tableware made of silver*
toxic – *poisonous*

See also: The Empire 6–7; Society 10–11; Literature 14–15; Art and Crafts 20–21

CASE STUDY

Afternoon tea

The ceremony of afternoon tea took place daily in most middle- and upper-class homes. It was a symbol of refinement. In upper-class homes, high tea was an occasion when servants would pour the tea for guests, using only the finest SILVERWARE and crockery.

> ▶ **Source: William Gladstone, 1865**
> The politician William Gladstone described the importance of tea for the Victorians:
>
> *"If you are cold, tea will warm you. If you are too heated, it will cool you. If you are depressed, it will cheer you. If you are excited, it will calm you."*

Afternoon tea for a middle-class Victorian family.

Health and Medicine

As the population grew, so did the spread of diseases. However, the introduction of ANTISEPTIC meant that fewer people died from infections after operations. The average lifespan increased as medical care and SANITATION improved.

DISEASES

Several 19th-century diseases produced the same symptoms of fever, headache, coughing and vomiting. EPIDEMICS of cholera and typhoid killed thousands, and people living in damp houses often contracted the lung disease tuberculosis (TB). Diseases that most affected children were chickenpox, diphtheria, measles, mumps, scarlet fever, whooping cough and poliomyelitis (polio), all of which could be fatal. People had to pay to see a doctor, so most illnesses were treated by a mother at home.

Everyone had their own home cures. Some people thought you could prevent colds by sewing children into brown paper vests smeared with thick lard.

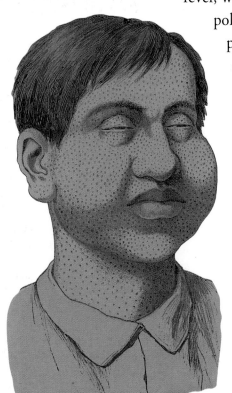

This cartoon shows an unfortunate man suffering from smallpox.

> ▶ **Source: Isabella Beeton, Mrs Beeton's Book of Household Management, 1861**
> Isabella Beeton wrote about protecting children from diseases:
>
> *"We see elaborate care bestowed on a family of children, everything studied that can tend to their personal comfort – pure air, pure water … despite of all this care and vigilance, disease and death invading the guarded treasure."*

26

MEDICAL PRACTICES

Health care and medicine in early Victorian times was often poor. Many doctors were poorly trained and did not understand the causes of disease, so they treated only the SYMPTOMS.

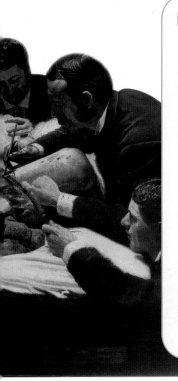

The Nurse, **by Sir Lawrence Alma Tadema, was painted in 1872.**

▶ **Source: 'A Few Hints on Health and Nursing', The Girl's Own Annual, 1885**

This was advice given on treating inflamed tonsils, which the Victorians called 'hospital throat':

"If taken at once, a 'hospital throat' can generally be cured by a simple GARGLE, chlorate of potash, port wine and vinegar, or even plain water… I saw a case of this kind … cured in one night by a very simple remedy: a gargle of brown sugar and vinegar."

Words to use in your project

anatomy – *the study of the body*
gruelling – *exhausting*
practitioner – *a person who is engaged in something*
prescription – *a medicine suggested by a doctor*
primitive – *ancient*

Glossary

antiseptic – *something that kills germs*
epidemics – *diseases caught by many people*
fallacy – *an incorrect belief*
gargle – *to wash the throat with a liquid*
sanitation – *healthy conditions*
symptoms – *signs of disease*

See also: The Victorians 4–5; Education 12–13; Significant People 18–19

CASE STUDY

Home remedies

The majority of people in the Victorian age depended on traditional remedies or herbal cures. Health advice was also obtained from household manuals. Nearly all manuals blamed the majority of illnesses on bad air and bad smells.

▶ **Source: Florence Nightingale, Notes on Nursing, 1860**

Florence Nightingale criticized this practice. She wrote:

"Another extraordinary FALLACY is the dread of night air. What air can we breathe at night but night air? … An open window most nights in the year will never hurt any one."

This painting, The Mission of Mercy, made in 1856 by Jerry Barrett, shows Florence Nightingale.

27

At Home

The homes of wealthy Victorians were large and surrounded by gardens. The middle-class population lived in comfortable town houses. Poor people lived in overcrowded TENEMENT buildings or small houses.

VICTORIAN HOUSES

More people moved into the towns and cities to work in factories. London, like most cities, was unprepared for this increase in people. People packed into crowded buildings. Private landlords built rows of small, cheap, brick houses to rent out. There was no indoor SANITATION and a whole street might share a few outside toilets and a pump. Water from the pumps was frequently POLLUTED. The homes of the middle and upper classes were better built, larger and often incorporated the latest GADGETS, including gas lighting, inside bathrooms and flushing toilets. These houses often had housekeepers.

▶ **Source: Isabella Beeton, Mrs Beeton's Book of Household Management, 1861**
Isabella Beeton wrote:

"… where there is a house steward, the housekeeper must consider herself as the immediate representative of her mistress, and bring, to the management of the household, all those qualities of honesty, industry, and vigilance …"

A typical Victorian house in Ironbridge, Shropshire.

COOKING AND CLEANING

All household chores were done by hand. Laundry was washed in a copper pot, put through a MANGLE and dried on a line. Ironing took hours because the iron had to be heated repeatedly over a fire. Cooking was done over an open fire or in a range cooker. The kitchen range had to be cleaned every morning, rubbed with black lead paste, polished and lit. Food was stored in LARDERS or in refrigerators towards the end of the Victorian era. In poor families children had to help with chores, while better-off families employed servants.

A Victorian refrigerator, about 1900.

Words to use in your project

enclosure – *an area of land surrounded by a fence or walls*
lodging – *a place to live*
prohibit – *to refuse to allow; ban*
tax – *money paid to the government*

Glossary

gadgets – *mechanical devices*
ghastly – *horrible*
in all conscience – *by any standard*
larder – *large cupboards for storing food*
mangle – *set of rollers used to remove water from laundry*
polluted – *dirty*
sanitation – *healthy conditions*
tenement – *a house divided into rooms to rent*

See also: Architecture 16–17; Work and Leisure 24–25

CASE STUDY

Urban life

At the start of the Victorian era people were either rich or poor. Then the middle classes developed and everyone hoped for a better lifestyle. Health improved as a comprehensive system of sanitation, including city sewers and pumping stations, was put in place. Even so, it seemed that many poor people were sinking further into degradation.

▶ **Source: George Sims, Horrible London, 1889**
In 1889 George Sims wrote about urban life for the poor:

"More than one-fourth of the daily earnings of the citizens of the slums goes over the bars of the public-houses and gin-places… that is a fact GHASTLY enough IN ALL CONSCIENCE…"

Only rich households had indoor flushing toilets.

Trade and Transport

Transport developed very rapidly during the Victorian era. First, roads were improved and then canals were built and finally railways were developed. These changes shortened travelling times and allowed goods to be sent around the country.

One of the strangest inventions of the era was the steam bicycle.

TRADE

In the 19th century, Britain led the world in trade. In the mid-1850s, exports to Asia were worth over £20 million. In 1848, Britain produced half the world's PIG IRON. Overseas INVESTMENT was vital to the nation's prosperity. The City of London quickly became the centre of the FINANCIAL world. Trade goods included cotton and other textiles from Britain's colonies. With Britain's FLOURISHING trade came unrest from dock workers, who demanded higher wages.

Tea clippers were an effective form of transport for international trade.

> ▶ **Source: Manchester Evening News, August 16, 1889**
> Chairman of the Dock Directors, Mr S Holland, said:
>
> *"What the cost would be of GRANTING the demands of the men, I cannot exactly say, but it would be at least £100,000 … We cannot afford an advance in wages … When the pinch comes, as come it must, the hopes of the strikers will receive a severe shock and I shall be surprised if there is any backbone left."*

TRANSPORTATION

By 1852, all Britain's main rail routes had been built. Train travel was cheaper than other forms of transport.

> ▶ **Source: Thomas Carlyle, from Letters and Memorials of Jane Welsh Carlyle, 1941**
>
> Author Thomas Carlyle described his first train journey:
>
> *"I was dreadfully frightened before the train started; it seemed to me certain that I should faint, from the impossibility of getting the HORRID thing stopped."*

For local travel, people used horses and wagons. In 1865, the first petrol-driven 'horseless carriage' appeared. In 1885, the 'safety bicycle', with two equal-sized wheels, was introduced.

Words to use in your project

combustion – *the process of burning*
ingenious – *clever and inventive*
magnitude – *extent*
signal – *a sign*
stagecoach – *a large closed horse-drawn vehicle*
standardize – *to regulate*
suburban – *beyond the city limits*

Glossary

financial – *related to money matters*
flourishing – *prosperous; successful*
granting – *agreeing to allow*
horrid – *unpleasant*
investment – *a money-making scheme*
pig iron – *iron made in moulds that look a bit like pigs*

See also: The Empire 6–7; Art and Crafts 20–21; At Home 28–29

CASE STUDY

The Great Exhibition

Queen Victoria's husband Prince Albert dreamed up the idea of a world fair – a showcase for industrial achievements. The Great Exhibition opened in London's Hyde Park on 1 May 1851. More than six million people from Britain and overseas came to see the 14,000 exhibits.

> ▶ **Source: Alfred, Lord Tennyson, Lines written to commemorate the Great Exhibition**
>
> Lord Tennyson wrote:
>
> *"…Steel and gold, and corn and wine,*
> *Fabric rough or fairy-fine, … a feast*
> *Of wonder, out of West and East …"*

This Owen Jones watercolour, The Great Exhibition, was painted in 1851.

Index

Victorian Timeline

1832
The Reform Act grants more men the right to vote and gives more MPs to the big cities. Parliament becomes more representative.

1833
The Factory Reform Act makes it illegal to employ children under nine in factories and limits the hours older children can work.

1837
Queen Victoria comes to the throne, aged 18. Isambard Kingdom Brunel builds the first passenger steamship to cross the Atlantic Ocean.

1840
Queen Victoria marries Prince Albert.

1847
Vanity Fair by William Makepeace Thackeray and Wuthuring Heights by Emily Brontë are published. Anne Knight proposes that women are given the vote. Chloroform is used as an anaesthetic.

1848
The Pre-Raphaelite movement begins.

1850
Most railway lines in Britain have been built by this date.

1851
The Great Exhibition opens.

1854–56
The Crimean War. Florence Nightingale improves conditions in the hospitals.

1859
Charles Darwin publishes The Origin of the Species, his theory of evolution.

1861
Prince Albert dies.

1865
Elizabeth Garrett Anderson becomes the first woman to qualify as a doctor.

1867
The Reform Act gives working men the right to vote, although the very poorest men are still excluded.

1868
The leader of the Liberal Party, William Gladstone, becomes prime minister for the first time.

1874
Benjamin Disraeli becomes prime minister.

1876
Queen Victoria is crowned Empress of India.

1880
William Gladstone becomes prime minister. The Education Act is passed, making school compulsory for all children aged 5–10.

1882
The Married Women's Property Act allows women to continue to own the property they held before marriage.

1901
Queen Victoria dies.